Dragons in Chinese Art

by HUGO MUNSTERBERG

March 23 through May 28, 1972

GALLERY HOURS
MONDAY THROUGH FRIDAY 10-5
SATURDAY 11-5
SUNDAY 2-5

*The Gallery will be closed
all Holidays*

CHINA HOUSE GALLERY ● CHINA INSTITUTE IN AMERICA
125 EAST 65th STREET, NEW YORK, NEW YORK 10021

CHRONOLOGY

Shang Dynasty 1523-1028 B.C.

Chou Dynasty 1027-256 B.C.
    Western Chou Dynasty 1027-771 B.C.
    Eastern Chou Dynasty 770-256 B.C.
        Period of Spring and Autumn Annals
        722-481 B.C.
        Period of Warring States 480-221 B.C.

Ch'in Dynasty 221-206 B.C.

Han Dynasty 206 B.C.-220 A.D.
    Western Han Dynasty 206 B.C.-9 A.D.
    Eastern Han Dynasty 25-220 A.D.

The "Six Dynasties" 265-589

Sui Dynasty 581-618

T'ang Dynasty 618-906

The "Five Dynasties" 907-960

Liao Dynasty 907-1125

Sung Dynasty 960-1279
    Northern Sung Dynasty 960-1127
    Southern Sung Dynasty 1127-1279
    Yuan Dynasty 1279-1368
    Ming Dynasty 1368-1644
    Ch'ing Dynasty 1644-1912

CATALOGS ALSO PUBLISHED BY CHINA HOUSE GALLERY

SELECTIONS OF CHINESE ART
by Mrs. Gilbert Katz
Oriental Department, Brooklyn Museum

ART STYLES OF ANCIENT SHANG
by Mrs. Llewellyn Young, *Asia Art Department*
Manhattanville College

ANIMALS AND BIRDS IN CHINESE ART
by Fong Chow, *Associate Curator-in-Charge*
Far Eastern Department,
The Metropolitan Museum of Art

GARDENS IN CHINESE ART
by Wango H. C. Weng

CHINESE JADES THROUGH THE CENTURIES
by Joan M. Hartman

FOREIGNERS IN ANCIENT CHINESE ART
by Ezekiel Schloss

CHINESE PAINTED ENAMELS
by J.A. Lloyd Hyde

ALBUM LEAVES
by C. C. Wang

MING PORCELAINS — A RETROSPECTIVE
by Suzanne G. Valenstein
Far Eastern Department,
The Metropolitan Museum of Art

CHINESE SILK TAPESTRY: K'O-SSU
by Jean Mailey
Textile Study Room,
The Metropolitan Museum of Art

EARLY CHINESE GOLD AND SILVER
by Dr. Paul Singer

We invite you to subscribe to the above. Unfortunately the catalogs on Gardens and Jades have been sold out.

© China Institute in America, 1971
    Library of Congress Catalog Card Number 73-186402

COVER:

Description on page 56

CHINA INSTITUTE ART COMMITTEE

JOHN M. CRAWFORD, JR., *Chairman*

MRS. EDWARD M. PFLUEGER, *Co-Chairman*

WANGO H. C. WENG, *Co-Chairman*

Fong Chow
Miss Louise Crane
Myron S. Falk, Jr.
Professor Wen Fong
Mrs. Benjamin Gim
Mrs. Alan S. Hartman
Su Chen Ho
Mrs. Gilbert Katz
Dr. Aschwin Lippe
Fritz Low-Beer

Miss Elizabeth Lyons
Professor Jane Gaston Mahler
Miss Jean Mailey
Paul E. Manheim
Dr. Chih Meng
Earl Morse
Miss Eleanor L. Olson
Mrs. Tsuyee Pei
Ezekiel Schloss
Miss Jean Schmitt
Miss Mary Ann Siegfried

Professor Alexander C. Soper III
Mrs. Edwin F. Stanton
Mrs. Charles J. Tanenbaum
LeMar Terry
Mrs. Murray A. Valenstein
Chi-ch'ien Wang
Gordon B. Washburn
Professor Chiang Yee
Mrs. Llewellyn Young

COURSES AT CHINA INSTITUTE

The School of General Studies of China Institute offers courses in Chinese Art, History, Culture, Philosophy, Music, Literature, Calligraphy, Painting, Cookery and other subjects.

China Institute is dependent upon its Associates for their annual support and on friends, corporations and foundations for contributions. Gifts to China Institute are deductible for federal income tax purposes. New friends are urged to make themselves Associates in one of the following categories: Associate $15.00; Contributing Associate $25.00; Supporting Associate $50.00; Fellow $100.00; Gallery Sponsor $500.00; Patron $1,000.00 or more.

China Institute is an educational institution chartered by the Board of Regents of the University of the State of New York. Non-profit and non-partisan, China Institute is supported by contributions and grants from individuals, corporations and foundations.

[3]

LENDERS TO THE EXHIBITION

Asian Gallery

The Brooklyn Museum

Professor and Mrs. Lawrence B. Cohen

Warren E. Cox and Associates

Mr. and Mrs. Myron S. Falk, Jr.

Fogg Art Museum

Mr. and Mrs. Fritz Low-Beer

The Metropolitan Museum of Art

Mr. and Mrs. Earl Morse

Professor and Mrs. Hugo Munsterberg

William Rockhill Nelson Gallery—Atkins Museum

The Art Museum, Princeton University

Museum of Art, Rhode Island School of Design

Seattle Art Museum

Mr. Laurence Sickman

Dr. Paul Singer

Mr. Frederick Wulsin

Yale University Art Gallery

SPONSORS OF CHINA HOUSE GALLERY

Mr. Avery Brundage

Mrs. C. Y. Chen

Mr. John M. Crawford, Jr.

Mr. Myron S. Falk, Jr.

Mr. and Mrs. Benjamin Gim

Mr. and Mrs. Alan S. Hartman

Mr. and Mrs. Abraham Hertzberg

The J. M. Kaplan Fund

Mr. and Mrs. William B. Jaffe

Mr. Henry Luce III

Mr. and Mrs. Paul E. Manheim

Mr. and Mrs. John C. Maxwell, Jr.

Mrs. Maurice T. Moore

Mr. and Mrs. Rafi Mottahedeh

Mr. Roy R. Neuberger

Mrs. Tsuyee Pei

Mrs. Edward M. Pflueger

Mrs. John D. Rockefeller 3rd

Mrs. Charles J. Tanenbaum

Mr. and Mrs. Hamburg Tang

Mr. and Mrs. K. K. Tse

Mrs. Dorothy Tsu

Mrs. Ho-Ching Yang

FOREWORD

DRAGONS IN CHINESE ART is the twelfth consecutive exhibition of classical Chinese Art to be presented by China House Gallery. Dr. Hugo Munsterberg, Professor of Oriental Art at New York State University College at New Paltz, New York, has assembled the exhibition and written the accompanying catalog, and to him the Trustees of China Institute express their deep gratitude. Dr. Munsterberg is the author of several books on the art of East Asia and a noted scholar and lecturer in this field.

Once again, China House Gallery is privileged to exhibit rare and valuable objects lent to us by museums and private collectors. To them we express our appreciation for their generosity. It is an honor to complement the work of the Institute in presenting the art of the East to our audience of the West in this distinguished fashion.

F. RICHARD HSU
President

IN APPRECIATION

I am deeply grateful to Mr. F. Richard Hsu, President of China Institute, and to the Art Committee of China House Gallery for giving me the opportunity to present this exhibition on Dragons. Such an exhibition would not have been possible without the cooperation of the many lenders, both public and private, who so generously allowed me to borrow from their collections, and the work of many colleagues and staff members of China Institute.

I must particularly mention Mrs. Edward M. Pflueger, whose thorough knowledge of printing has done so much to assure the high quality of the Gallery catalogs, and Brigid Kernan, Program Assistant, who has worked with me throughout the planning of the exhibition. I am indebted to Cleo Nichols and LeMar Terry for expert installation and lighting. The photographers whose fine work appears in the catalog are Sean Kernan (cover), Thomas Feist, G.D. Hackett, John D. Schiff and Otto E. Nelson.

Hugo Munsterberg

INTRODUCTION

One of the most popular of all the symbolic animals which occur in Chinese art is the dragon, or *lung.* This fabulous creature, however, is by no means limited to the Far East. As the famous Argentine writer Jorge Borges says in his *Book of Imaginary Beings,* "We are ignorant of the meaning of the dragon in the same way that we are ignorant of the meaning of the universe, but there is something in the dragon's image that fits man's imagination, and this accounts for the dragon's appearance in different places and periods."[1] Dragon myths and records of dragons exist in almost all ages and civilizations. Even though the specific meaning of the dragon image varies from place to place and often changes drastically over the years, the general ideas associated with dragons are very similar. To quote Mircea Eliade:

> Dragons, snakes, shellfish, dolphins, fish and so on are the emblems of the water; hidden in the depths of the ocean, they are infused with the sacred power of the abyss; lying quietly in lakes or swimming across rivers, they bring rain, moisture, and floods, thus governing the fertility of the world. Dragons dwell in the clouds and in lakes; they have charge of thunder bolts; they pour down water from the skies, making both fields and women fruitful."[2]

In the West the dragon is usually associated with the forces of evil while in China and Japan he is thought of as auspicious. His general appearance, however, is surprisingly similar in both regions, for the dragon is usually described as a ferocious, four-footed animal with sharp teeth, wings at the shoulders, and the tail of a snake. Here is a description of the mysterious *lung* by the Chinese dragon painter Tung Yü:

> "There is a difference between the male and the female dragon. The male has horns and his body always writhes violently. He has deep-set eyes, wide-open nostrils, a pointed beard and compact scales. The body is strong toward the head and diminishing toward the tail. He is red as fire, grand and beautiful. The female dragon has no horns and her body forms quite flat waves. The eyes stand out, the muzzle is cut straight, the mane curly, the scales sparse, and the tail is stronger than the body."[3]

[1] J.L. Borges: *The Book of Imaginary Beings,* New York, 1969, p. 13.
[2] M. Eliade: *Patterns in Comparative Religion,* New York, 1963, p. 207.
[3] O. Sirén: *Chinese Painting,* Vol. II, New York, 1958, p. 149.3

Numerous accounts of the appearance of dragons exist both in the East and the West, some of them surprisingly recent. In Europe we are told that a dragon was sighted flying from Mount Pilatus in Switzerland in 1649,[4] and in China a dragon is said to have been seen as late as 1931 emerging from the Kan River in Kiangsi province. Although the dragon as such is purely imaginary, there is little doubt that the idea can be traced back to some real animal, probably one existing in prehistoric times, the memory of which was preserved in what Jung calls the collective unconscious of the human race. All kinds of different animals have been suggested by the many scholars who have speculated about dragons and dragon lore, including snakes, lizards, crocodiles, and water monsters. Just what the origin of this myth was will probably never be known, but it is interesting to note that Chinese archaeologists have recently found fossil remains of pterosaurs, warm-blooded flying reptiles existing between ninety and a hundred million years ago, which had a ten-foot wing span and a brain equal to that of modern birds. No doubt it was this kind of creature or a similar prehistoric animal whose huge size and ferociousness gave rise to the dragon myths.

The earliest appearance of the dragon in art occurs in ancient Mesopotamia where the Sumerians describe the monster Kur as a dragon-like creature. In Babylonia, Tiamut, the goddess of the sea, is represented as a dragon who is killed by Marduk whose attribute the dragon then becomes. He personified the fertilizing action of the waters and it is he who makes the plants grow and the grain ripen, indicating that in those early times the dragon was already associated with water and fertility. The earliest artistic representations of these concepts are found in the cylinder seals of the ancient Near East, some of which go back as far as the fourth millenium B.C. The best known portrayal of the dragon in ancient Mesopotamian art is found on the Ishtar Gate of sixth century Babylon where the dragon and the bull are represented, both of which were sacred to Marduk. No doubt the numerous references to dragons in the Old Testament are derived from these sources—in fact Nebuchadnezzar, King of Babylon, to whose palace the Ishtar Gate leads, is referred to as a dragon who devoured Israel. And it is probably from ancient Assyria and Babylonia that the Romans derived their dragon standards and the people of the Byzantine Empire their dragon banners. The dragon in medieval art and legend is believed to come from both Roman and Biblical sources. It is already represented on one of the shields found at the Anglo-Saxon ship burial at Sutton Hoo, and a dragon plays a prominent role in *Beowulf.* The dragon is a recurrent element in Christian legend. It stands for the forces of evil, and one of the most common themes is the hero who comquers the dragon, as in the well-known story of Saint George.

[4] R.W. Chambers: *Beowulf,* Cambridge, 1959, p. 11 (footnote).

It is not known just what the connection is between the Chinese dragon and that of the ancient Near East. No dragons appear in the art of prehistoric China, and since there is much evidence for influences from Mesopotamia and Iran reaching ancient China, it does not seem unlikely that the dragon concept was derived from Western Asia where it occurred almost two thousand years before it appears in China. The oldest Chinese dragons date from Shang times, around the middle of the second millenium B.C. The character for dragon is already used on the oracle bones of the Shang period, and there are references to dragons in the earliest Chinese literary works such as the *I Ching*, or Book of Changes, in which the dragon is associated with the dynastic rulers, the *Shih Ching*, or Book of Songs and the *Shu Ching*, or Book of History, in which there are numerous references to dragon banners and to robes with dragon designs.

The physical appearance of the dragon, or *lung*, has been endlessly discussed by both Western and Chinese scholars. Some, such as Florence Waterbury, have even suggested that there is no real dragon in Shang art. According to Chinese texts, the dragon has the head of a horse, the tail of a snake, wings on his sides, and four legs, each foot having four claws, or five in the case of imperial dragons. It was believed that the dragon had the power to alter its size at will, becoming exceedingly large or infinitesimally small, and that he could make himself visible or invisible. Bernard Karlgren distinguishes between various kinds of dragons such as winged, feathered, gaping, vertical, and trunked. Other authors have suggested that one cannot really distinguish clearly between the dragon, the snake, and the mysterious animal called *kuei,* a one-legged monster mentioned in some Chinese texts. Although it is impossible to give an exact description of an imaginary animal, there is no doubt that such a beast did exist in the thought and art of early China.

Two dominant ideas were associated with the dragon. On the one hand he is a dynastic emblem symbolizing the royal house and the power of the kings. On the other hand he is the animal of the sky, representing clouds, rain, and lightning. It is reported that one of the ancestors of the first Chinese house, the Hsia dynasty, transformed himself into a dragon in a holy place. Dragons appeared when there was a renewal or a decline of the generic virtue by which the Hsia dynasty was empowered to reign. One branch of the family had the privilege of breeding dragons and knew the art of making them thrive, while another Hsia ruler fed upon dragons to make his reign prosperous. Dragons were also seen as the progenitors of royal ancestors, and it is reported that a dragon appeared at the time of Confucius' birth which was interpreted as an auspicious sign. According to legend, when Confucius met Lao-tzu, he remarked to his disciples that he had seen the dragon. It is also said that a dragon emerged from the Yellow River to reveal the famous circular diagram symbolizing the reciprocal play of the Yang and the Yin. Finally, the Chinese emperor was often said to have a dragon face, and he was seated on a dragon throne dressed in a dragon robe.

The second idea associated with the dragon, that of insuring the fertility of the fields, is a concept which in China was closely connected with the imperial house, for it was the ruler who produced harmony between Earth and Heaven, thereby assuring prosperity and a good harvest. The altar devoted to the worship of ancestors stood to the east of the royal palace, the direction of spring, which was symbolized by the Green Dragon. But above all the dragon was the emblem of the sky, inhabiting the clouds and pouring rain on the parched earth. It is this aspect of the dragon that is most common both in Chinese literature and art. A tempest in the sky indicated that the celestial dragons were engaged in a fight, and it was believed that the dragon god was the deity responsible for storms and rain. As such he could be a beneficial power bringing the water needed for a good harvest, but if not treated with the proper respect, he could turn into a destructive force causing drownings and floods.

These ancient concepts going back to the very beginnings of Chinese history were still widely held in modern China where it was believed that dragon deities inhabited the lakes and rivers and that four dragon kings dwelling in crystal palaces were lodged in the depths of the seas. Offerings to dragons are even reported in our own time and according to popular folklore, dragons controlling rivers often exact the sacrifice of a victim as an offering to insure their goodwill. To this day Chinese communities throughout the world celebrate the dragon festival on the fifth day of the fifth month with dragon boat races, and fancy dragon boats are carried to the shore and burned. An enormous dragon made of linen, bamboo, and paper is borne in procession through the streets of the towns on the fifteenth day of the first month. In front of it a ball is held which, according to de Groot, is the sun which the Azure Dragon swallows at the beginning of spring. In times of drought Chinese villagers made clay dragons which they hoped would cause rain, and they brought offerings and said prayers at the local temples dedicated to the dragon gods. To this very day, in both China and Japan, the dragon is considered the most auspicious of the animals which symbolize the twelve year cycle. In this role, the dragon is called *ch'en* instead of the usual term *lung*. A person born in the year of the dragon is believed to be particularly fortunate for the dragon is a superior being which brings good luck—in fact, it is one of the twelve lucky symbols in Chinese art.

The dragon has always been one of the most popular of the animals represented in Chinese art, starting in Shang times and continuing right down to the commercial art of the present. Only the neolithic pottery of the prehistoric period, although it represents snakes, does not have any creatures which can be clearly identified as dragons. However, beginning with the Shang period (c. 1500 — c. 1000 B.C.), numerous representations of dragons appear on all kinds of objects. Sometimes they form the main decorative motif, but more often they are part of a larger iconographic whole. Although there is still a good deal of uncertainty about the exact meaning of the animal forms on the ceremonial vessels and other objects from early China, there can be no doubt, as Carl Hentze has demonstrated in a number of books, that they were symbolic in nature and served magical purposes connected with the worship of divine ancestors and the forces of nature, with both of which the dragon is closely associated.

In the Chou period (c. 1000 — c. 200 B.C.), the use of dragons became even more common. Not only did they occur as decorative motifs on many of the bronze vessels, they were also an intricate part of the abstract decorative designs which were so common, especially during the Late Chou period, and through which they found their way by means of the nomad tribes of the steppes into the Barbarian art of the Germanic and Celtic people. As painting and sculpture emerged as major art forms, the dragon began to be treated as a separate subject. A magnificent example is the Late Chou bronze dragon in the Stoclet Collection in Brussels, and then there are the marvelous jade dragons in various public and private collections. Dragons were painted on the walls of palaces and temples, often, according to Chinese texts, to avert a drought and produce rain. None of these have survived, but the dragons on lacquer vessels and ceramic objects give us some idea of what these paintings must have been like.

With the Han period (c. 200 B.C. — 200 A.D.), the dragon became primarily associated with the animals of the four directions — the *Ssu Shên* as they are called in Chinese. In this role the dragon is the symbol of the East, while the tiger represents the West, the bird the South and the tortoise and snake the North.[5] This motif was particularly common as a decorative design for mirrors, and it continued to be popular for a thousand years, from Han to late T'ang times. In addition to the mirrors, all kinds of Han objects have elegant dragon designs. Lacquer tables such as the beautiful example in the Fogg Museum, a great variety of boxes, ceramic vessels and textiles all show the gracefully undulating forms of dragons which were a favorite subject with Han craftsmen and consequently were used over and over again. Although few painted dragon designs of Han date survive, there can be no doubt from the stone engravings and impressed tiles that dragons were often shown in the pictorial art of the Han period. In sculpture, too, dragons were frequently represented in stone, clay and above all, bronze.

[5] H. Munsterberg: "The Symbolism of the Four Directions in Chinese Art," *The Art Quarterly,* Spring, 1951, pp. 33-42.

After the introduction of Buddhism during the early centuries of the Christian era, the traditional Chinese dragon became confused with the *naga* image of India for which the term dragon is employed in China. Although both are associated with water, rivers, lakes, and sea, their meaning and derivation is actually quite different. In contrast to the Chinese *lung*, the Indian *naga* is clearly a snake, often specifically shown as a cobra which was looked upon as a sacred earth and water deity in India and Southeast Asia long before it became incorporated into Buddhist iconography. Since the two concepts were quite similar, it is not surprising that the same dragon form was usually used for both, in spite of their different meaning.

Beginning with the Six Dynasties period (265–589) and especially during T'ang (600–900) and Sung times (960–1280), dragon painting became very popular, with some painters making their reputation entirely in this field. Among them was the sixth century artist Chang Sêng-yu who executed a wall painting with four dragons. When viewers complained that he had left out the eyes, the master resumed his work, adding eyes to two of the painted figures. It is said that immediately the air was filled with thunder and lightning, the walls cracked and the dragons ascended to heaven while the two to which he had not given eyes remained on the wall. It is also said that the famous eighth century painter Wu Tao-tzu painted dragons on the palace walls from which vapor and mist emanated whenever it was going to rain.[6] Unfortunately neither of these early works has survived, but there are some provincial versions of dragon painting on the walls of a Korean tomb which may suggest something of the dynamic energy and expressive power which these works must have had.

The most famous dragon painter was the thirteenth century artist Ch'ên Jung, who lived during the Southern Sung period. Numerous works in both Western and Chinese collections are traditionally attributed to him. The most celebrated is the Nine Dragon scroll in the Boston Museum of Fine Arts which is one of the masterpieces of Chinese painting in America. Among the other works ascribed to him, the finest is the fragment of a larger scroll, now in the Nelson Gallery in Kansas City, whose splendid brush work suggests the hand of the master. Other Sung artists who represented dragons were the famous Ch'an master Mu Ch'i and the numerous Buddhist painters who portrayed dragons in the company of Lohans.

During the later Chinese dynasties, the dragon became particularly popular as a decorative motif. Although literary references indicated that dragon robes were given to

---

[6] O. Sirén: *Chinese Painting* Vol. I, New York, 1958, p. 110.

Chinese officials above the third rank by the T'ang empress Wu as early as 694 and dragon designs are frequently found on lacquers, porcelains and metal work of earlier periods, they do not become really common until Ming (1368-1644) and Ch'ing times (1644-1912). The textiles often used the dragon emblem as the dominant motif, and it was considered a great honor for a court official to be presented with a dragon robe by the emperor. While few Ming robes have survived, dragon robes from Ch'ing times are fairly common, and they are among the masterpieces of the textile artists of traditional China. That this design was also widely used in the Ming period is indicated in the ancestor portraits which show the deceased in their court robes.

Other art forms which use the dragon again and again are the porcelains and lacquers of the Ming and Ch'ing period. No animal was more popular for none lends itself better to decorative design than the dragon with its graceful form and undulating movement. It is represented on dishes, plates, jars, vases, and even garden seats and writing boxes, now in blue on a white ground, now in bright enamel colors, and now merely incised in the ceramic surface. Sometimes, no doubt, it stood for either the emperor or the sky and at other times it was probably only a decorative motif, but its popularity indicates the important place this legendary being had in the hearts and minds of the Chinese people.

BIBLIOGRAPHY

J.L. Borges: The Book of Imaginary Beings, New York 1969
S. Cammann: China's Dragon Robes, New York 1952
V.B. Dennys: Folk Lore Of China, London and Hongkong 1876
M.W. De Visser: The Dragon in China and Japan, reprint Wiesbaden 1969
H. Frankfort: Cylinder Seals, London 1929
M. Granet: Chinese Civilization, London 1930
J. Hackin (editor): Asiatic Mythology, London 1932
C. Hentze: Funde in Alt-China, Göttingen 1967
E. Ingersoll: Dragons and Dragon Lore, New York 1927
B. Karlgren: Yin and Chou in Chinese Bronzes, BMFEA No. 8
A. Marcus: Der Blaue Drache, Zürich 1949
O. Sirén: Chinese Painting, New York 1958
E. Smith: The Evolution of the Dragon, Manchester 1919
E.T.C. Werner: A Dictionary of Chinese Mythology, Shanghai 1932
F. Waterbury: Early Chinese Symbols and Literature, New York 1942

1. TING
Shang Dynasty, 1523-1028 B.C.
Bronze
H. 6½"

The important role the dragon played in Chinese culture is well indicated by the central position the dragon motif has in this splendid ceremonial vessel in which it no doubt stands for the dragon deity associated with heaven, rain and fertility.

Dr. Paul Singer

[13]

←

2. SPATULA
Shang Dynasty, 1523-1028 B.C.
Bone
L. 9¼"

Dragon designs are used as ornamental motifs in many different kinds of implements and artistic media as seen in this bone spatula from Shang times.

Published: Catalog of the Singer Collection at Asia House Gallery, New York, 1965, No. 17.

Dr. Paul Singer

3. WINE-STIRRING IMPLEMENT   →
Shang Dynasty, 1523-1028 B.C.
Bronze
H. 5½"

Although the form of the dragon varies greatly from period to period and from object to object, the main idea of the swirling dynamic forms expressive of the forces of the celestial realm is forcefully expressed in this implement probably used for stirring the sacred wine for the ritual ceremonies.

Dr. Paul Singer

[14]

4. CHARIOT ORNAMENT
Shang Dynasty, 1523-1028 B.C.
Bronze
L. 14"

Since the dragon was an emblem of power it often appears on chariots and weapons, no doubt because it was thought to give protection and success in battle.

Dr. Paul Singer

5. HORSE BITS
Shang Dynasty, 1523-1028 B.C.
Bronze
D. 5"

Horse bits in ancient China were often decorated with symbolic animal designs and served purely decorative as well as more practical purposes.

Dr. Paul Singer

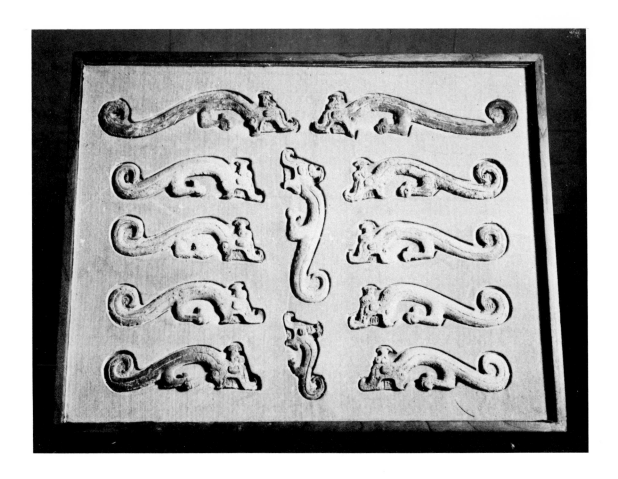

6. FITTINGS FOR A CHARIOT
Shang Dynasty, 1200 B.C., from An-Yang
Bronze

A. L. 4⅜″ H. 1¼″
B. & C. L. 4¾″ W. 1¼″
D. L. 5″ W. 1¼″
E. L. 6¼″ W. 1⅜″
F. L. 2½″ W. 1⅛″
G. L. 4⅝″ W. 1⅜″

H. L. 4½″ W. 1¼″
J. L. 4⅝″ W. 1⅜″
K. L. 4½″ W. 1¼″
L. L. 4⅝″ W. 1¼″
M. L. 6⅛″ W. 1¼″

In many instances ancient Chinese objects of art have not only one single dragon or a pair of dragons, but many representations of the dragon motif hoping thereby to enhance the auspicious forces emanating from this sacred form.

Nelson Gallery-Atkins Museum

[16]

7. PENDANT
Middle Chou Dynasty, 10th-7th century B.C.
Jade
L. 2⅜" W. 1¾"

For those who are sceptical about the essentially symbolic and sacred meaning of the designs in ancient Chinese art this jade carving should be particularly interesting, for it shows the dragon supporting and upholding a human figure who should be looked upon as a sky deity or a divine ancestor of the Chou people.

Seattle Art Museum
Eugene Fuller Memorial Collection

8. ORNAMENT
Eastern Chou Dynasty, 770-256 B.C.
Jade
L. 6″

Dr. Paul Singer

Dragon ornaments made of jade such as these two splendid Late Chou pieces were probably attached to the robes of priests or high officials as emblems of power and rank as we find them embroidered on the dragon robes of later times.

9. ORNAMENT
Eastern Chou Dynasty, 770-256 B.C.
Jade
L. 2″

Dr. Paul Singer

10. CUT-OUT ORNAMENT
Eastern Chou Dynasty, 770-256 B.C.
Stone
L. 5" W. 4½"

The dragon design often appears in a very abstract and stylized form which is hardly recognizable unless the eye is trained to detect the swirling, dynamic forms associated with the magic animal.

Dr. Paul Singer

ll. SCABBARD CHAPE
Late Chou Dynasty, 770-256 B.C.
Jade
L. 2"

Dr. Paul Singer

The sword furniture of ancient China was often decorated with dragon designs as is beautifully illustrated by these two fine jade scabbard sections from the Singer collection.

12. SCABBARD FITTING
Late Chou Dynasty, 770-256 B.C.
Jade
L. 3½"

Published: Catalogue of exhibition of "Early Chinese Jades," University of Michigan, Ann Arbor, 1933, No. 119.

Dr. Paul Singer

13. VASE
Late Chou Dynasty, 480-
221 B.C. or Han Dynasty,
206 B.C.-220 A.D.
Pottery
H. 14" D. (top) 4½"
D. (bottom) 5⅞"

The dragon, in either
incised or painted form,
was a favorite deco-
rative design occurring
on pottery jars during
Late Chou and Han
times, as is well illus-
trated by this powerful
jar from the Seattle
Museum.

Seattle Art Museum

Eugene Fuller Memorial
Collection

14. DRAGON FIGURE
Later Han Dynasty, 25-221 A.D.
Pottery with traces of polychrome
L. 8⅝″ H. 5½″

The dynamic, animated form of the dragon lends itself particularly well to sculptural representation as is clearly seen in this fine ceramic sculpture of the Late Han period.

Mr. Laurence Sickman

15. WELL HEAD
Han Dynasty, 206 B.C.-220 A.D.
Clay
L. 9"

In Han times the dragon appears more and more as one of the symbols of the four directions, representing the East in contrast to the tiger who represents the West, two contrasting forms confronting each other as shown in this well head.

Dr. Paul Singer

16. TOMB TILE
Han Dynasty or earlier
Gray pottery
L. 26½" H. 24⅜"

Tomb tiles of ancient China, although humble productions of mere artisans, often reflected, as this design does, the pictorial designs of the Chinese painters of their period and help to give us a good idea of the greatness of this now largely lost art.

Nelson Gallery
Atkins Museum

17. PI-SHAPED DISK
Early Han Dynasty, 206 B.C.-9 A.D.
Jade
D. 2½"

Published: Singer, P., "Unique Object in Oriental Art," ORIENTAL ART, 1961.

Dr. Paul Singer

These circular disks known as Pi were regarded as symbols of heaven but may originally have been solar emblems since they resemble the archaic character of the sun. The dragon as the ruler of the sky is seen here dominating the heavenly sphere.

18. PI-SHAPED DISK
Early Han Dynasty, 206 B.C.-9 A.D.
Jade
D. 2¾"

Mr. and Mrs. Myron S. Falk, Jr.

19. DRAGON FIGURE
Later Han Dynasty, 25-220 A.D.
Gilded bronze
L. 3½"

Among the most appealing of all representations of dragons are the small but fanciful gilded bronze dragons of Han times, of which this is a fine example.

Dr. Paul Singer

20. COFFIN WEIGHT
Early Han Dynasty, 206 B.C.-9 A.D.
Bronze
H. 2¼" D. 2¾"

The exact use to which this metal weight was put is not known with certainty but it has been suggested that it might have served as a coffin weight.

Fogg Art Museum
Paul J. Sachs Bequest

21. STONE RUBBING
Han Dynasty, dated 171 A.D.
Rubbing on paper
H. 53¾″ W. 40″

In ancient times long before photography was invented, the standard way of reproducing works of art, especially stone engraving and low relief sculptures, was the rubbing executed in black on white paper.

Fogg Art Museum

22. DRAGON FIGURE
Six Dynasties, 220-589
Clay
H. 12½″ L. 13″

Of all the splendid dragons in American collections, this magnificent Wei dragon from the Rhode Island School of Design Museum is one of the finest and we are particularly proud to include it in this exhibition.

Museum of Art
Rhode Island School of Design

23. DRAGON FIGURE
Six Dynasties, 265-589
Gilt bronze
H. 4³/₁₀″ L. 6⁷/₁₀″

Another superb example of dragon sculpture in American museum collections is this vibrant, animated gilded bronze dragon in The Art Museum at Princeton University.

The Art Museum
Princeton University

24. DRAGON HEAD
Six Dynasties, 3rd-4th century A.D.
Painted pottery
H. 3¼″ L. 4½″

Sculptured animal heads such as this were often made separately and might then be attached to a body made of a different material or used by themselves to stand for the entire animal.

Mr. Laurence Sickman

25. FINIAL
Six Dynasties, 265-589
Gilt bronze
H. 1½″ L. 2½″

This charming gilt bronze dragon head probably served as a finial for some ornamental staff or decorative element.

Fogg Art Museum
Meta and Paul J. Sachs Bequest

[29]

26. JAR
Six Dynasties, 265-589
Clay
H. 9¼″

This motif of the sculptured dragon form winding its way around the neck of a jar is first seen in this period and becomes very popular in Sung times.

Dr. Paul Singer

27. STELE RUBBING
Six Dynasties, 265-589
Rubbing on paper
H. 88″ W. 39″

This rubbing taken from a Buddhist stele of the Northern Chou Dynasty shows how the typically Chinese dragon motif finds its way even into Buddhist art when it really had no place in traditional Buddhist iconography.

Fogg Art Museum

28. MIRROR
T'ang Dynasty, 8th century
Bronze with silver
D. 12¼"

The material splendor of the T'ang civilization and the powerful artistic style of the age is well illustrated by this splendid mirror with a dragon design from the Nelson Gallery.

Nelson Gallery—Atkins Museum

29. TILE
T'ang Dynasty, 618-906
Pottery
D. 7¼"

Pottery roof tiles were often decorated with dragon designs in the hope that this sacred animal connected with rain and water would protect the building against fire.

Asian Gallery

[33]

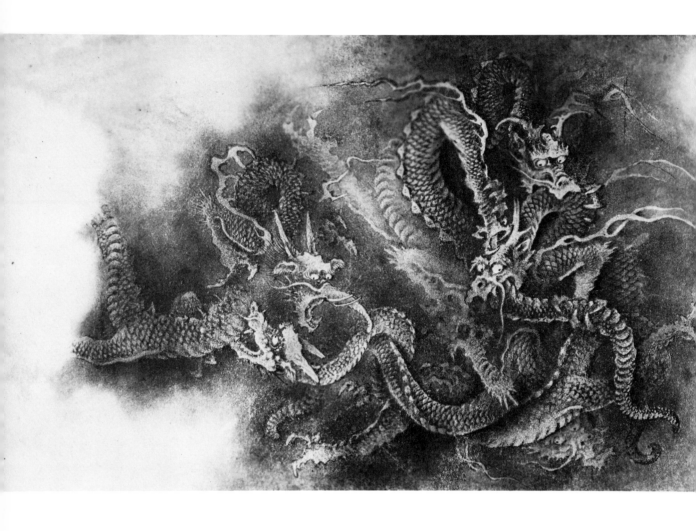

30. HANDSCROLL
Attributed to Ch'ên Jung, Sung Dynasty, middle 13th century
Ink on paper
H. 13½" L. 23½"

Of all the many dragon paintings attributed to Ch'ên Jung, the most celebrated dragon painter of China, this is, next to the magnificent dragon scroll in the Bostom Museum, the finest and should be considered to be by the hand of the famous master himself.

Published: Sirén, O., *Chinese Painting*, Volume III., pl. 360.

Nelson Gallery—Atkins Museum

[34]

31. SCROLL
Attributed to Ch'ên Jung, Sung Dynasty, middle 13th century
Ink on paper
H. 17½" W. 75½"

Another example of Ch'ên Jung's celebrated dragon scrolls is this version in the Metropolitan Museum which may not be by the master himself but is certainly very close to his style and may have been painted by one of his immediate followers.

Published: Chow, F., *Animals and Birds in Chinese Art,*
China House Gallery, 1967, pl. 44.

The Metropolitan Museum of Art
The H.O. Havemeyer Collection
Bequest of Mrs. H.O. Havemeyer, 1929

32. CELADON FUNERAL JAR
Sung Dynasty, 960-1279
Porcelain
H. 10½"

The dragon design was a favorite decorative motif among the Sung potters, executed in sculptural form, as is seen in this example, or in low relief, incised or painted form.

Seattle Art Museum
Eugene Fuller Memorial Collection

33. TZ'U CHOU JAR
Sung Dynasty, 960-1279
Stoneware
H. 12¾"

Although executed by a potter rather than by a professional painter, this bold dragon painting is worthy of one of the great painters of China and shows how the high level of artistry characteristic of Sung painting is reflected in the decorative arts.

Warren E. Cox and Associates

34. STEM CUP
Yuan Dynasty, 1279-1368
Porcelain
H. 3⅝"

This exquisite example of a Yüan period blue and white stem cup is one of the earliest examples of dragon representations in blue and white porcelains.

Published: *Chinese Art Under the Mongols,* The Cleveland Museum of Art, 1968.

Mr. and Mrs. Myron S. Falk, Jr.

35. CELADON BOWL
Yüan Dynasty, 1279-1368
Porcelain
D. 5⅜"

While most decorations on Yüan porcelains take the form of painted designs executed in cobalt, the animated dragon form is applied in low relief on the surface of this vessel.

Mr. and Mrs. Myron S. Falk, Jr.

[39]

36. SCROLL
Ming Dynasty, Ch'ên Jung tradition
Ink on paper
H. 13³/₅" W. 26'5²/₅"

Since Ch'ên Jung enjoyed a tremendous reputation as the outstanding dragon painter of China, he inspired many imitators during subsequent periods. Among these later versions, this long and well-preserved scroll in The Art Museum at Princeton is the most handsome and complete.

Published: Rowley, G., *Chinese Painting,* Princeton, 1947.

The Art Museum
Princeton University

37. DRAGON
Ming Dynasty, 1368-1644
Bronze
H. 15½" L. 19½" W. 10"

In later ages when the magic associated with the dragon in ancient China had lost some of its power, the animal was no longer quite as convincing and powerful as in earlier times. It, nevertheless, was often represented in sculpture as well as painting and especially in the decorative arts.

Yale University Art Gallery
Gift of Mrs. William H. Moore for the Hobart Moore
and Edward Small Moore Memorial Collection

38. DRAGON FIGURE
Ming Dynasty, 1368-1644
Jade
L. 4⅝" H. 2¼"

Seattle Art Museum
Eugene Fuller Memorial Collection

The dragon, which had been so popular in Late Chou jades, also frequently occurs in the jades of the Ming period when an archaistic revival of interest in early Chinese art became the vogue among scholars and connoisseurs, as well illustrated in these Ming examples.

39. PLAQUE
Ming Dynasty, 1368-1644
Jade
H. 4" L. 6½"
Seattle Art Museum
Eugene Fuller Memorial Collection

40. BOX WITH COVER
Ming Dynasty, Hsuan-te period, 1426-1435
Porcelain
H. 1½″ D. 3½″

Usually the painted dragon designs are only found on one side of a box or vessel, but in this interesting early Ming example the same animated dragon form is repeated at the bottom of the porcelain box as well.

Warren E. Cox and Associates

41. STEM CUP
 Ming Dynasty, Chia-ching period, 1522-1566
Porcelain
H. 4¼"

Here dragons and clouds representing the celestial realm indicate clearly that to the Chinese of later times the dragon was primarily the ruler of heaven, inhabiting the sky and controlling the rains.

Fogg Art Museum
Bequest of Samuel C. Davis

[44]

42. IMPERIAL VASE
Ming Dynasty, Chia-ching period, 1522-1566
Porcelain
H. 8"

Over and over again the craftsmen decorating the numerous porcelain jars and vases produced by the great porcelain factories of Ming China employed the dragon as the dominating motif in their painted designs, indicating the popularity the dragon enjoyed even during this late period.

Seattle Art Museum
Eugene Fuller Memorial Collection

43. JAR WITH COVER
Ming Dynasty, probably
Wan-li period, 1573-1620
Porcelain
H. 4$^7/_{10}''$ D. 4$^7/_{10}''$

The Brooklyn Museum
Bequest of Augustus S. Hutchins

Although no two dragon designs are exactly alike, since they were individually painted, nevertheless, they are often very similar, suggesting that they were the products of the same workshops or even produced by the same hand.

44. JAR
Ming Dynasty, probably
Wan-li period, 1573-1620
Porcelain
H. 5$^5/_8''$

Fogg Art Museum
Bequest of Samuel C. Davis

45. JAR
Late Ming Dynasty, 1573-1619
Porcelain
H. 21″ D. 19″

These large blue and white jars with bold dragon designs are very characteristic of the late
Ming period, especially of the reign of the emperor Wan-li (1573-1619).

The Brooklyn Museum
Bequest of Augustus S. Hutchins

46. JAR
Late Ming Dynasty, 17th century
Porcelain
H. 5⅛″

As so often happens in Chinese ceramics, the reign mark found on the bottom of this vase dating it in the Hsuan-te period (1426-1435) does not correspond to its actual date which is seventeenth century.

Professor and Mrs. Hugo Munsterberg

47. BRUSH REST
Ming Dynasty, Wan-li period, 1573-1620
Porcelain
H. 4⅛″

Among the many interesting porcelain implements employed by the Chinese scholars, this brush rest decorated with dragons is one of the most fascinating.

Seattle Art Museum
Eugene Fuller Memorial Collection

48. TZ'U CHOU JAR
Ming Dynasty, 1368-1644
Stoneware
H. 16½″

This Ming Tz'u Chou jar forms an interesting contrast with the Sung Tz'u Chou jar from the same collection also shown in this exhibition, illustrating the decline which painting had experienced in the intervening centuries.

Warren E. Cox and Associates

49. BOX
Ming Dynasty, early 15th century
Carved lacquer
H. 2¾" D. 7 ¹/₁₆"

Although lacquers with dragon designs are common, early Ming examples such as this are very rare and we are fortunate indeed to be able to include it in this exhibition.

Published: Low-Beer, F., "Chinese Lacquer of the Early 15th Century," B.M.F.E.A., No. 22, Fig. 19.

Exhibited: Mostra d'Arte Cinese, Venice, 1954, cat. No. 734.

Mr. and Mrs. Fritz Low-Beer

50. PANEL
Ming dynasty, 1368-1644
Lacquer
H. 7⅛" W. 7⅛"

From the collection of Mr. Frederick Wulsin
Courtesy of the Fogg Art Museum

The dragon is a favorite decorative motif of the Ming lacquer artists and recurs over and over again with only slight variations in form on the numerous dishes, boxes, plates and plaques produced during this period.

51. DISH
Ming Dynasty, Chia-ching period
1522-1566
Lacquer
D. 7¼"

Mr. and Mrs. Myron S. Falk, Jr.

[51]

52. TABLE
Ming Dynasty, Wan-li period, 1573-1620
Lacquer
L. 6'3" W. 3'

The dragon, in addition to being used on small lacquer objects, is sometimes also found as the major ornamental form on large pieces of furniture such as tables, chests and cupboards, as is seen in this splendid late Ming example.

Asian Gallery

[52]

53. TRAY
Ming Dynasty, Tien-ch'i period, 1623
Lacquer
L. 13¼″ W. 4¾″

This late Ming tray is interesting not only for its splendid dragon designs, but also for its swastikas showing that this ancient solar symbol was known in China long before it became associated with National Socialist Germany.

Mr. and Mrs. Fritz Low-Beer

54. DISH
Ming Dynasty, Wan-li period, 1592
Carved Lacquer
D. 15″

This fine carved cinnebar lacquer plate decorated with seven medallions of Imperial dragons pursuing flaming pearls is fully discussed in Low-Beer, "Chinese Lacquer of the Early 15th Century," B.M.F.E.A., No. 22.

Exhibited: "Mostra d'Arte Cinese," Venice, 1954, cat. no. 734.

Mr. and Mrs. Fritz Low-Beer

55. BOWL
Ch'ing Dynasty, K'ang-hsi period, 1662-1722
Porcelain
D. 7½"

The last great period of Chinese ceramics was the long and glorious rule of the emperor K'ang-hsi when the art of porcelain manufacture attained its ultimate perfection. This fine blue and white bowl is an excellent example of this art.

Professor and Mrs. Lawrence B. Cohen

56. VASE
Ch'ing Dynasty, K'ang-hsi period, 1662-1722
Porcelain
H. 10⅞"

This elegant K'ang-hsi vase well illustrates the level of perfection in potting and painting achieved by the best of the Ch'ing potters.

Published: Exhibition catalogue of Chinese Ceramics, Los Angeles County Museum, Los Angeles, 1952.

Mr. and Mrs. Myron S. Falk, Jr.

57. DISH
Ch'ing Dynasty, K'ang-hsi period, 1662-1722
Porcelain
H. 1¾" D. 8⅝"

In addition to the fine blue and white vases produced by the K'ang-hsi potters, some of the finest of the porcelains of the Ch'ing period were decorated in enamel colors over the glaze of white, of which this is a very fine example.

The Metropolitan Museum of Art
Rogers Fund, 1922

58. CELADON PILGRIM BOTTLE (on cover)
Ch'ing Dynasty, Ch'ien-lung period, 1735-1795
Porcelain
H. 8¾"

This splendid pilgrim bottle, also reproduced in color on the cover of the catalog, indicates how even in the eighteenth century the Chinese potters were still capable of doing outstanding work.

Mr. and Mrs. Earl Morse

[56]

59. VASE
Ch'ing Dynasty,
Ch'ien-lung period,
1735-1795
Porcelain
H. 12½"

While painted designs
in cobalt blue under
the glaze or in enamel
colors over the glaze
were the standard way
of decorating Ch'ing
porcelains, this delicate
incised dragon design
on a Ch'ien-lung vase
shows how skillfully
this technique was
also employed.

Mr. and Mrs. Earl Morse

60. PLATE
Ch'ing Dynasty, Yung-chêng period,
1723-1735
Porcelain
D. 6¾"

The brief rule of the emperor Yung-chêng, although less illustrious than that of his predecessor K'ang-hsi or his successor Ch'ien-lung, nevertheless produced some fine porcelains of which this is a good example.

Mr. and Mrs. Myron S. Falk, Jr.

61. BOWL
Late Ch'ing Dynasty, 19th century
Porcelain
H. 3" D. 8¼" Base 2⅞"

A piece from the very end of the Ch'ing Dynasty, this porcelain bowl shows how the dragon motif continued to be popular in Chinese ceramics even in this late period. In fact, it continues to be used even today.

Fogg Art Museum
Gift of Miss Louise W. Case

62. PLAQUE
Ch'ing Dynasty, Ch'ien-lung period,
1736-1795
Jade
H. 4³/₁₆″ W. 4″

Seattle Art Museum
Eugene Fuller Memorial Collection

These very late eighteenth century jades executed in a very detailed and realistic style are typical of the type of dragon representation found in the jades of the Ch'ing period.

63. WATER POT
Ch'ing Dynasty, Ch'ien-lung period,
1736-1795
Jade
H. 4⅞″ W. 9″

Seattle Art Museum
Eugene Fuller Memorial Collection

64. SEAL
Ch'ing Dynasty, 1644-1912
Ivory
H. 1¼″

This charming little seal with a dragon design carved in ivory is typical of the kind of implement used by the scholars of traditional China.

Dr. Paul Singer

65. SCREEN
Ch'ing Dynasty, Ch'ien-lung period, 1736–1795
Jade
H. 8¹¹/₁₆″ W. 4¹/₁₆″

This jade screen with its delicate incised double dragon shows what a fine sense of line and design the Chinese craftsmen possessed even during the late period.

Seattle Art Museum

Eugene Fuller Memorial Collection

[60]

66. STAND
Ch'ing Dynasty, 19th century
Silvered bronze
H. 7″ L. 10⁴⁄₅″

This large, swirling dragon holding the crystal ball on his claw indicates that even during the nineteenth century the magic of this mysterious animal still had a great hold with the Chinese popular imagination.

The Brooklyn Museum
Friedsam Bequest

67. BELL
Ch'ing Dynasty, 1644-1912
Bronze
H. 8½"

This bell, executed in an archaeistic style based on Late Chou models, shows that the ancient bronze forms with their dragon designs enjoyed great popularity even in this late period.

Yale University Art Gallery
Gift of Mr. and Mrs. George Fitch